WINGS OF WAR

Fighter Planes of World War II

by Nancy Robinson Masters

Content Review:
Research Department
Unites States Air Force Museum

CAPSTONE BOOKS

an imprint of Capstone Press
Mankato, Minnesota

Capstone Books are published by Capstone Press
151 Good Counsel Drive, P.O. Box 669, Mankato, Minnesota 56002
http://www.capstone-press.com

Library of Congress Cataloging-in-Publication Data
Robinson Masters, Nancy.
    Fighter planes of World War II/by Nancy Robinson Masters.
        p. cm.--(Wings of war)
    Includes bibliographical references and index.
    Summary: Introduces various kinds of fighter planes used by the Army Air
Force and by the Navy and Marines during World War II, their missions, and the
weapons employed.
    ISBN 1-56065-533-X
    1. Fighter planes--United States--History--Juvenile literature.
2. World War, 1939-1945--Aerial operations, American--Juvenile literature.
[1. Fighter planes. 2. Airplanes, Military. 3. World War, 1939-1945--Aerial
operations.] I. Title. II. Series: Wings of war (Mankato, Minn.)
UG1242.F5R66   1998
623.7'464'097309044--DC21

                                                    97-5999
                                                      CIP
                                                       AC

The author would like to thank Harry Wadsworth, Laura Thaxton, and Bill
Masters for their research assistance.

Editorial credits
Editor, Matt Doeden; cover design, Timothy Halldin;
    illustrations, James Franklin; photo research, Michelle L. Norstad

Photo credits
American Airpower Heritage Museum, 18, 22
Archive Photos, 4, 7, 35
Lockheed Martin Skunk Works, cover, 11
National Archives, 12, 30, 38, 41
Real War Photos, 32
Larry Sanders, 8,14, 20, 25, 26, 28, 29, 36, 42

TABLE OF CONTENTS

CHAPTER ONE

World War II Fighters

In the late 1930s, the German military had the most powerful air force in the world. German leader Adolf Hitler tried to conquer Europe with this air force. Conquer means to defeat and take over an enemy.

World War II began when the German military invaded Poland in 1939. A group of countries called the Allied nations tried to stop Germany and the Axis powers. The Allied nations wanted to keep the Axis powers from

In the late 1930s, the German military had the most powerful air force in the world.

moving further. The Allied nations included Canada, England, France, and Russia. The Axis powers were the German, Japanese, and Italian militaries.

In 1941, the Japanese military attacked Pearl Harbor, Hawaii. There was a United States Navy base at Pearl Harbor. The attack brought the United States into World War II. The United States joined the Allied nations.

Air Fighting History

Fighting with airplanes began in World War I (1914-1918). Pilots flew in open-cockpit airplanes. An open-cockpit airplane has no roof above the pilot's seat. At first, pilots dropped bricks on enemy troops. Then they began carrying guns to shoot at enemy airplanes.

Pilots learned to fly behind enemy airplanes to shoot them down. This became known as pursuit fighting. Pursuit is the act of chasing an enemy. Pilots also used pursuit tactics in World War II (1939-1945). Tactics are plans

Pilots learned to fly behind enemy pilots to shoot them down.

for fighting a battle. Today's fighter pilots still use pursuit tactics.

Little Friends

World War II fighters were small and fast. Most bombers were large. Most bombers were slower than fighters. A bomber is an airplane that drops bombs. Bombers depended on fighters for

Most World War II bombers were large.

protection when they went on bombing
missions. A mission is a military task. Fighter
pilots flew above, below, and beside bombers
as escorts. An escort is a fighter that flies
with a bomber to protect it. Fighter escorts
attacked enemy aircraft that tried to shoot
down the bombers.

Bomber pilots called fighters Little Friends. Escort fighters worked in teams. A bomber could have as many as four groups of escort fighters. Bombers started missions with one group of escort fighters. Sometimes a second group of fighters took over if the first group had to get fuel. The second group came from a different base or ship. When bombers returned from their missions, another group of fighter escorts protected them. If that group of fighters ran out of fuel, a new group took over.

Attack

World War II fighter pilots did not always wait for enemy aircraft to attack. Sometimes pilots flew fighters to high altitudes and dove on enemies below them. Altitude is the height of an object above the ground. Dive flaps on fighters' wings helped slow the dives. This gave pilots time to get enemy planes in sight.

Sometimes fighter pilots tricked enemies. They flew over enemy airfields before bombing missions. They forced enemies to send fighters in pursuit. The enemies' airfields were left without protection. Then bombers bombed the airfields.

Reconnaissance Missions

Fighters also flew reconnaissance missions. Reconnaissance means gathering information about an enemy. Fighter pilots flew both photo-reconnaissance missions and tactical-reconnaissance missions.

Pilots took photographs of enemy targets during photo-reconnaissance missions. The U.S. military could plan missions by using these photos. Pilots often flew airplanes called P-38 Lightnings for photo-reconnaissance missions. P-38 Lightnings could fly as high as 25,000 feet (7,620 meters).

Fighter pilots observed enemies during tactical-reconnaissance missions. Pilots became skilled at spotting enemy weapons on the ground. The pilots reported where they saw enemy weapons and bases. Pilots often used North American P-51 Mustangs for tactical-reconnaissance missions.

Pilots flew P-38 Lightnings for photo-reconnaissance missions.

The P-61 Black Widow flew night missions.

Night Fighters

Some fighters flew night missions. Northrop P-61 Black Widows flew at night. Douglas A-20 Havocs had bright searchlights in their noses. Pilots used the lights to search for enemy targets at night.

Night fighters had two seats. One seat
was for a pilot. The second seat was for a
radar operator. A radar operator uses radar.
Radar is machinery that sends out radio waves
to locate objects.

CHAPTER TWO

Fighter Weapons

Fighter airplanes had more weapons than other airplanes. Fighters had machine guns, cannons, bombs, and explosive rockets.

Machine Guns

Most World War II fighters had .50 caliber Browning machine guns. Caliber is the size of a bullet. A larger caliber number means a larger bullet. A .50 caliber bullet was one-half inch across. A .50 caliber Browning machine gun could fire 800 bullets per minute. It weighed only 65 pounds (29.5 kilograms). These guns were

Most World War II fighters used machine guns that fired .50 caliber bullets.

mounted on fighters' fuselages or wings. A fuselage is the long body of the plane that carries the cargo and crew.

Pilots used three kinds of bullets in World War II machine guns. Armor-piercing bullets could punch through the metal parts of an airplane. Tracer bullets left trails of smoke that showed pilots where to shoot. Incendiary bullets started fires wherever they hit.

Most fighters had fixed guns. A fixed gun is aimed in one direction and cannot move. Pilots with fixed guns had to fly directly at the aircraft they were shooting.

Cannons

The smallest cannon on U.S. fighters was the 20 millimeter cannon. Cannons shot shells. Cannon shells were larger than bullets. The Lockheed P-38 Lightning was one kind of fighter with a 20 millimeter cannon.

Some cannons could fire shells weighing more than one pound (.45 kilograms). These

The P-38 Lightning had a 20 millimeter cannon.

were 37 millimeter cannons. One kind of 37 millimeter cannon was the M-4. M-4 cannons could fire shells greater distances than any other World War II cannons. The Bell P-39 Airacobra had M-4 cannons.

MAJOR PACIFIC AIR BATTLES OF WORLD WAR II

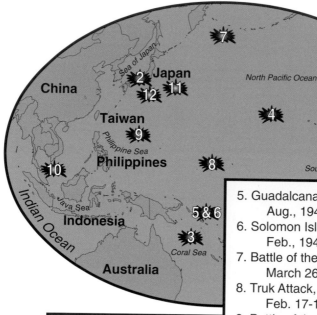

5. Guadalcanal Campaign,
   Aug., 1942 - Feb., 1943
6. Solomon Islands Campaign,
   Feb., 1943 - Nov.,1944
7. Battle of the Komandorski Islands,
   March 26, 1943
8. Truk Attack,
   Feb. 17-18, 1944
9. Battle of the Philippine Sea,
   June 19-20, 1944
10. Battle of Leyte Gulf,
    Oct. 23 - 26, 1944
11. Battle for Iwo Jima
    February, 1945
12. Atomic Bomb dropped on Hiroshima
    August 6, 1945

1. Pearl Harbor,
   Dec. 7,1941
2. Doolittle Raid
   April 18,1942
3. Battle of the Coral Sea,
   May 4-8, 1942
4. Battle of Midway,
   June 3-6, 1942

Bombs

Some fighters carried bombs. A P-51 Mustang could carry 2,000 pounds (900 kilograms) of bombs. A Navy F4U Corsair fighter-bomber could carry 4,200 pounds (1,890 kilograms) of bombs.

A fighter could not move quickly when it carried bombs. The extra weight made it slower. Other fighters had to protect fighters carrying bombs.

Rockets

Some American fighters were armed with explosive rockets near the end of World War II. Rockets were lighter than bombs. They could travel faster and farther. The P-51 Mustang was one kind of plane armed with rockets.

Rockets were carried in tubes beneath the wings. Fighters with rockets could hit enemies that were far away. They did not have to fly over enemies like bombers did.

CHAPTER THREE

Air Force Fighters

The U.S. Army Air Forces fought on every front of World War II. A front is a place where militaries are fighting. Manufacturers built planes for many missions. They built many kinds of fighters. These fighters each had strengths and weaknesses.

Lockheed P-38 Lightning

Lockheed designed the P-38 Lightning pursuit fighter in 1937. It had two engines

The P-38 Lightning had two engines and two tails.

and two tails. Enemy pilots called it the forked-tail devil. The P-38 Lightning was the first American airplane to destroy a German aircraft during World War II. The P-38 was also one of the airplanes the Army Air Forces used for reconnaissance.

The United States built 9,942 P-38s for the war. They were among the best-known fighters of World War II.

Bell P-39 Airacobra

Some pilots called the Bell P-39 Airacobra the best low-altitude fighter of the war. The P-39 could dive fast, but it turned slowly. It had an in-line engine behind the pilot. An in-line engine has its cylinders in a straight row. A cylinder is a tube-shaped part of an engine that fills with gas and air. The cylinders are where an engine's power is produced.

The P-39 Airacobra had an in-line engine behind the pilot.

The P-39 had a 37 millimeter cannon. It had four .50 caliber guns and could carry 500 pounds (227 kilograms) of bombs.

Allied Russian pilots often flew Airacobras. Alexander Pokryshkin was the most successful P-39 pilot. Pokryshkin flew P-39s in 47 of his 59 air victories.

Bell P-63 Kingcobra

The Bell P-63 Kingcobra was a later model of the Bell P-39 Airacobra. The Kingcobra had longer wings and a larger tail than the Airacobra. The Kingcobra also carried rockets. The Allies built more than 3,600 Kingcobras during World War II.

The United States never used Kingcobras in battle. Russia used about 2,000 Kingcobras. France used about 300.

The P-63 Kingcobra was a later model of the P-39.

Curtiss P-40 Warhawk

The Curtiss P-40 Warhawk was the first U.S. fighter available in large numbers. Between 1940 and 1942, the United States built more

Warhawks than all other fighter types combined. The United States built more than 13,000 Warhawks during World War II.

Members of the American Volunteer Group used P-40 Warhawks. The American Volunteer Group helped defend China from Japanese attacks. The members of the American Volunteer Group were called Flying Tigers.

The Flying Tigers had shark teeth painted on the noses of their Warhawks. The Flying Tigers shot down 286 Japanese airplanes in World War II. Enemies shot down only eight Flying Tigers.

Pilots could not see over a P-40 Warhawk's nose when it was on the ground. Pilots needed help when moving a P-40 Warhawk on the ground. Someone had to sit on a wing to warn pilots about anything in their way.

The Flying Tigers had shark teeth painted on the noses of their P-40 Warhawks.

Republic P-47 Thunderbolt

Pilots called the Republic P-47 Thunderbolt the Jug. Some called it the flying milk bottle because of its shape. It was the largest single-engine fighter used in World War II. The P-47 Thunderbolt had a radial engine. A radial engine has its cylinders arranged in a circle.

P-47 Thunderbolts were known for their diving ability. They were also among the

sturdiest airplanes used in World War II. P-47
Thunderbolts had armor. Armor is a protective
metal covering. P-47s could take a lot of
enemy fire and keep flying.

North American P-51 Mustang
The United States planned, built, and flew the
first North American P-51 in just 117 days. The
Mustang was the best high-altitude, long-range
fighter of World War II.

Pilots called the P-47 Thunderbolt the Jug.

Allies used the P-51 Mustang for tactical reconnaissance. It was also an excellent combat airplane. P-51 pilots destroyed seven enemy airplanes for every P-51 destroyed by enemies.

Northrop P-61 Black Widow

The Northrop P-61 Black Widow was the first American aircraft built just for night fighting. It had seats for a pilot, a radar operator, and a gunner.

Black Widows were large airplanes. Their wings stretched 66 feet (20 meters) from tip to tip. They carried radar in their noses. The radar could locate enemy airplanes within ten miles (16 kilometers).

Black Widows carried four fixed 20 millimeter cannons. They could carry 6,400 pounds (2,880 kilograms) of bombs. All of these airplanes were black. Some Black Widows were used as reconnaissance planes after World War II.

The P-51 was flown for tactical reconnaissance.

CHAPTER FOUR

Navy and Marine Fighters

The U.S. Navy and Marines also used fighters during World War II. Many fighters were based on aircraft carriers in the Pacific Ocean. The Navy and Marine fighters protected ships and attacked enemies. They also protected Navy and Marine bombers.

Grumman F4F Wildcat
The Grumman F4F Wildcat was a single-engine fighter built for the U.S. Navy. Wildcat

The U.S. Navy and Marines also used fighters during World War II.

pilots could take off from small aircraft carriers. They sank Japanese submarines. Some Wildcat pilots flew reconnaissance missions.

The Wildcat's main rival was a Japanese plane called the Zero. The Wildcat was not as quick as the Zero. But it was sturdier. The Wildcat also had larger guns than the Zero.

Grumman F6F Hellcat

The Grumman F6F Hellcat replaced the F4F Wildcat. The Hellcat became the most successful plane on the Pacific front. The Hellcat had an 18-cylinder radial engine. It was larger and more powerful than the Wildcat. The Hellcat carried 400 shells for each of its six machine guns. Some Hellcats carried rockets.

The United States built more than 11,000 Hellcats. Hellcat pilots could defeat Japanese Zero pilots easily. Many people think Hellcats kept the Japanese military from winning the war.

The Hellcat was the most successful airplane on the Pacific front.

Vought F4U Corsair

The United States built more Vought F4U Corsairs than any other kind of fighter plane. The United States built about 12,500 Corsairs during World War II.

The Corsair could take off from land or from aircraft carriers. The Corsair combined a sturdy frame with a powerful engine. It could reach altitudes higher than 30,000 feet (9,144 meters).

The Corsair could serve as a bomber. It could carry bombs and rockets. It could also be a reconnaissance plane. Corsairs were so successful that the United States made them until 1952.

The United States built about 12,500 Corsairs during World War II.

CHAPTER FIVE

German and Japanese Fighters

American planes helped the Allies defeat the Axis powers in World War II. But some famous fighter planes came from Germany and Japan.

A6M Zero

The most famous Japanese World War II plane was the Mitsubishi A6M. Allied pilots called the A6M the Zero. The Zero had small guns and no armor.

The most famous Japanese World War II airplane was the A6M Zero. This Zero was captured by the U.S. military.

The Zero was successful early in World War II. It was a good combat plane because it was so light. It was quick and it turned easily. No American plane could turn as easily or quickly.

The Zero was one of the most successful airplanes on the Pacific front until 1943. In 1943, the United States introduced the Grumman F6F Hellcat. The Hellcat was more powerful than the Zero.

Messerschmitt Me-109

The Messerschmitt Me-109 was the most successful German fighter plane during World War II. Germany built almost 35,000 Me-109s. The Me-109 was armed with a 30 millimeter cannon and four 20 millimeter machine guns. It could not carry much fuel. It could not stay in the air as long as many other planes.

The most successful pilot in history flew Me-109s. He was a German pilot named Erich Hartman. Hartman shot down 352 enemy planes during his military career.

Germany built almost 35,000 Me-109s.

Focke Wulf 190

The German air force built the Focke Wulf 190 (FW-190) to help the Mc-109. The FW-190 was small and fast. It could fly up to 453 miles (729 kilometers) per hour.

The FW-190 had four fixed machine guns. It could carry bombs. Some FW-190s carried rockets. Germany built more than 20,000 FW-190s for World War II.

tail

tailwheel

P-40 Warhawk